RESOLVE YOUR FEARS:

Activate Your Spiritual Immune System

RESOLVE YOUR FEARS:
Activate Your Spiritual Immune System

Rev. Dr. Michelle Medrano

FOREWORD
BY DR. ROGER TEEL

Park Point
PRESS

Park Point Press | 573 Park Point Drive | Golden CO 80401

Park Point Press
573 Park Point Drive
Golden, CO 80401-7402
720-496-1370

www.csl.org/en/publications/books
www.scienceofmind.com/publish-your-book

Printed in the United States of America
Published March 2021

Editor: Julie Mierau, JM Wordsmith
Design/Layout: Maria Robinson, Designs On You, LLC

ISBN ebook: 978-0-917849-93-0
ISBN paperback: 978-0-917849-92-3

Dedication

I dedicate this book to COURAGE—the courage of humans throughout our history who have beaten the odds, taken the risks to love, to dream, to grow. They represent the true human spirit.

I specifically dedicate this book to my MOTHER, Linda Frazee, my son, Jesse Wentker, and my wonderful husband, Kenneth Crismon, who call me into fearless living every day. I am so grateful.

ForeworD

For God has not given us the spirit of fear;
but of power and of love and of a sound mind.

— 2 Timothy 1:7

This glorious truth shouts at us from the pages of this life-changing book by Dr. Michelle Medrano. I met Michelle in the early 1980s and was immediately captivated by her determination, natural wisdom, and fun-loving spirit. I watched her enthusiastically master the teachings that permeate the material you're about to read. She then charted a courageous course that took her from serving as an administrative assistant in our office to her heights now as a leading and highly respected New Thought spiritual leader. From the wealth of her personal and professional experience comes this fine guidebook for returning to our birthright as beings of power, love, and sound mindedness.

Fear is a frequent traveling buddy on everyone's life journey. Even the most accomplished or enlightened people have had to transcend enormous fears, so none of us should feel embarrassed or inadequate when we, too, become anxious or frightened. Dr. Michelle likens our liberation from the stranglehold of fear to unleashing the healing powers of the human body. Just as caring for the body tends to prevent disease, we also need inner self-care to thwart debilitating fears.

In this superb book, Dr. Michelle provides profound yet practical insights to help us realize a higher truth: Fear can grow us rather than shrink us, empower us rather than imprison us, and impel us rather than paralyze us.

History demonstrates that humanity is engaged in a crucial quest for an evolutionary shift: to transform the suffering and violence caused by a worldview that is deeply fear-based—and to reveal the peace, prosperity, and possibilities within an awakened and love-based awareness.

Dr. Michelle, my cherished friend and colleague, you are moving this mission forward powerfully. I have witnessed your beautiful spirit and your endless determination to transcend your own fears. Congratulations for bringing us this roadmap that leads us from the wastelands of fear back to our homeland in the healing power of our individual and collective hearts.

DR. ROGER TEEL
Author & Spiritual Leader
Minister Emeritus, Mile Hi Church

Acknowledgments

When I was a child, the sound of my grandfather's typewriter clicking away was a regular sound in my grandparent's home. That sound seems to have woven its way into my soul. In the modern world, it is the click of a keyboard on a computer. Yet, I give thanks that writing and books were in important part of my early life. I watched my grandfather write, and I read voraciously. Books have also been a huge part of my personal and spiritual life. Words that rose off the pages of sacred texts, self-help books, and spiritual writings have become a foundational part of who I am. Thank you to books and the authors who created them.

The love of books combined with my love of growing and deepening have motivated me to step forward to become an author. Thank you to my family of origin, my family of choice, and my spiritual family in the communities I have been blessed to serve. I have learned so much about life and love in family. My fondest hope is to give back in meaningful ways to those who have blessed me so greatly.

IntroductioN

In May 2019, I joined a writing workshop. The goal of the workshop was to write a book that a reader could pick up and read in three hours or less. Of course, one of the first tasks was to choose a topic to write about.

I have long imagined a world free of needless fear. I have imagined humans surrendering unconscious and conscious fears to live their best lives. Therefore, I set out in the workshop to capture my heart about freedom from fear.

When the workshop was complete, I spent months working on my manuscript, as many authors do. There were times the manuscript sat untouched for long periods of time. There were times when my personal editing was voracious.

Then, in the spring of 2020, not quite a year after the initial writing, the COVID-19 pandemic broke out all over the world. There were great racial tensions and protests in the United States. Wildfires and hurricanes struck countries around the world with a ferocity not previously experienced. The U.S. presidential election captivated Americans, creating tension and fear.

Fear broke out in great abundance. Clearly it was time to publish this book.

This is a basic book designed to challenge us to rise up and out of our individual and collective fear and live with greater courage. Conditions do not cause fear. Our thoughts, feelings, and beliefs about conditions cause us fear. We may not be able to change the conditions in which we find ourselves, but we can change our inner environment as we deal with those fears.

Just as we do things to build our physical immune system, we can build our spiritual immune system and move forward with courage and strength through that which we fear. My fondest hope for all of my human family is that we free ourselves to rise up.

Table of Contents

1   FEAR: ALIEN INVADER — PAGE 1

2 TOXIC RELEASE — PAGE 17

3 COURAGE IS BONE MARROW — PAGE 33

4 GET A SPIRITUAL SPLEEN — PAGE 47

5 WHITE LIGHT CELLS — PAGE 61

conclusion   **THE END OF FEAR** — PAGE 71

about the AUTHOR   — PAGE 75

RESOLVE YOUR FEARS:

Activate Your Spiritual Immune System

Our physical bodies contain antibodies found in our immune system. They combine with substances the body recognizes as alien, such as bacteria, viruses, and foreign substances, in our blood to keep our immune system strong. In our awareness, fear can be akin to a "foreign substance." It exists like a virus that invaded our world, our collective psyche, and our personal choices. We can create antibodies in our awareness that connect with our fear and help to dispel or heal it in our lives.

FeaR:
AlieN InvadeR

How the Immune System Works

Our physical immune system keeps our body healthy and strong. There are five main elements of the immune system. Ideally, we can be exposed to a virus, bacteria, toxins, or certain cells of disease and our immune system can easily fight them off and maintain our health.

Every day our bodies are exposed to viruses and diseased cells. Yet the stronger our immune system is, the healthier we are.

Healthy Fear

We do not need to abandon fear completely. There are times when our fear serves us. We might experience real live danger. Our intuition or senses can serve us and get our attention with fear rising. The adrenaline rush we get when we actually need to pay attention to some danger can help us stay safe.

For eons humans have had to manage intense danger from the animal kingdom, nature, and other beings. While these elements of life still exist and can represent challenges for us, we have learned to build cities, shelter, and negotiate with our words.

During the winter of 2019, Colorado's weather manifested with great intensity at times. Many times, the newscasters screamed, "An even bigger storm ahead!" They bantered about new definitions of storms, such as "Snowmagedden!," "Bomb Cyclone," and "Explosive cyclogenesis." Being proactive and "safe," schools sent kids home and businesses prepared for the worst. Some heavy snow fell and some tree branches fell. The weather brought some intense snows with wind. A few cars slipped and slid on the roads. Yet, for longtime Colorado residents, it seemed like . . . winter. The news channels appeared to be competing for viewership by inciting fear. They succeeded, as fearful residents stocked up on food and water.

We get caught up in our culture searching for truth and untruth. When they say something on television or on social media, we tend to believe it. "They" often appear to be overly motivated to get our attention and influence us. The main tool used to do this—fear.

Conscious Fears

We should be aware of things we know we are afraid of, such as spiders, snakes, heights, or horror films. Being consciously aware of things we are afraid of can help us make conscious choices about avoiding or healing those fears.

If those fears cause us great discomfort or emotional pain, we can learn to overcome and master them to achieve greater balance.

Humans can be courageous. Stories abound about people who overcome their deepest fears. Whether profound phobia or little irritations, we have the ability to free ourselves from our fears.

Unconscious Fears

Our awareness records every experience in this lifetime. In that recording, our awareness captured plenty of moments steeped with fear and cataloged them into our deeper mind. They are still active in our experience. Though we may not consciously understand why we fear rooms painted green, for example, our unconscious mind remembers. This realm of our mind contributes to the bulk of our fear-based awareness. Stress we cannot quite account for, emotionality we cannot explain, anxiety we cannot match with our current life experience are the result of the memories of the deeper mind that never forgets and wants to warn us to watch out.

The Virus of Fear

Just as we are exposed to physical viruses every day, we also get exposed to fear every day. Fear acts as a constant virus that broadcasts into our culture. We are encouraged to be afraid of the weather, the traffic, our neighbors, the terrorists, the IRS, the government, disease, aging, illness—and on and on and on. Fear can be so prevalent that we can become a bit desensitized to it. Just like a person who overuses antibiotics and finds themselves challenged to fight off an illness when it arrives, the virus of fear has over taken our world, and our ability to transcend it can be challenged.

Constant Feeling of Danger

This undercurrent of fear can create a feeling of constant danger. We can become hyper vigilant, which can feel and be unduly stressful. To feel and imagine danger around every corner can be exhausting. Yet many people live this way each day. Statistically, none of us are ever in as much danger as we imagine, yet our imaginations can run wild.

Fight-or-Flight Stress

The constant envisioning or imagining the dangers of our life causes us to go into the feeling of fight or flight. This means our nervous system may be constantly poised to fight off something or run away from something. With healthy fear, these chemicals serve us well. In daily life when we do not need them, they create great stress. When the alien invasion of fear takes hold, we get caught in the cycle.

Sharing the Virus with Others

Though we have the best intentions not to give people that flu we caught, sometimes we spread our germs and others get ill around us. The same can be true with this fear virus. We can infect those around us when we speak about our fears and encourage them to be afraid too. Or we can quietly spread the fear to our family and friends as they sense it or as they sense our stress levels. Just as we may have unconsciously absorbed the fears of our parents, our children can unconsciously absorb our fears.

My mother had the blessing of a mischievous brother six years her elder. While growing up, I repeatedly heard stories of how my uncle liked to play jokes on his little sister and cause her to react dramatically. When she was six years old, while sitting in the backseat of the family car, her brother threw a plastic snake on her. She panicked, screamed, and basically freaked out. This emotional experience set her up to be extremely diligent and not just afraid of snakes but panicked at even the thought of one. That fear stayed with her as she grew older. When she told us this story, we felt her fear and could see the panic in her eyes even just speaking about snakes.

As the child of a mother with a snake phobia, I noticed that even though my uncle never threw a snake on me, and no one else had done that to me in my life ever, and I had never even really seen a snake up close and personal, I also had a basic phobia about snakes. As I matured and felt this fear, I began to ask myself why.

I realized I just accepted and inherited my mother's fear. My imagination of what she went through felt alive in my body and my consciousness. Yet, as I deeply questioned myself, I began to see that I really don't feel that same level of fear of snakes. I don't love them, and I would likely not choose one for a pet, yet my authentic stance remains mostly free of fear about them. I am fairly "snake neutral." I had just taken on my mother's fear and lived from and reacted from it for many years.

What other fears had I inherited? This snake story helped me see that others can pass their fears on to us with repetition and intense energy. However, we don't have to take them on and accept them as ours.

Antibodies in Our Awareness

The most popular strategy for dealing with fear can be to simply ignore it or push it away or down. Yet just as the physical immune system meets the bacteria and faces it with antibodies for healing, we can create antibodies in our awareness or consciousness to meet the virus of fear when it shows up. We can transmute it.

Our new strategy must be one of conscious awareness of a fear taking hold and meeting the fear head on. Again, if we are in danger, we need to react. Yet most of our perceptions of danger live in our imagination.

Real or Imagined?

I heard a teaching story about a town where numerous people died of the plague. As a man walks on a path outside of the town, he sees the plague sitting on the side of the road. The man exclaims, "Hey, you are the plague! You just killed thousands of people in my town!" The plague replies, "I killed 100 people in your town. Fear killed the rest." Much of what we fear begins in our imagination and sets off the chemistry of weakness in some realm of our being, which can lead us into some unfortunate experiences. Just as weakness in our physical immune system can make us more vulnerable to colds and flu, weakness in our emotional immune system can make us more vulnerable to the fear flu.

Do Something

There are times when the fear we feel issues an invitation to handle something. We may need to have a conversation, or make an appointment, or handle a task. Fear can be a great excuse for procrastination.

Resolving fear and doing that which we are afraid to do can feel extremely empowering. Many risk takers attest to the feeling of fear being a part of the process of conquering a new experience—and they don't let the fear stop them.

We face risks every day. We drive on roads with busy traffic and face the potential of mishaps. We fall in love and face heartbreak. We fly on planes 30,000 feet in the sky. Some of us play sports and face physical danger in the process. In the extreme, some of us jump out of planes, go rock climbing, and race cars. We often *Feel the Fear and Do it Anyway,* the title of author Susan Jeffer's great book.

Heal Something

From a personal growth standpoint, fear exists most often as an invitation to heal something. Just as we have to be aware that if we have a cold we need to stop and rest and heal to get well. If we refuse, our illness gets worse. The presence of the virus of fear can be an invitation to stop and take care of our heart, mind, or soul. If we refuse, our experience of life can suffer greatly as our resistance to do that inner work causes us to feel a great disconnect from our ability to be centered, connected, and empowered. This becomes the point where we can be unpredictable and tempted to act in ways that are not in alignment with who we know ourselves to be or choose to be.

For some strange reason, I am a fan of shows that are about solving crimes. I find the forensic investigations fascinating. In a show called the "First 48," the creators believe investigators have a greater statistical chance of solving a crime if they can do it the first 48 hours after the crime has occurred.

During the show they interview victims and suspected perpetrators of all sorts of crimes—mostly murder. I am struck by the fact that most of the crimes they highlight have, at their core, fear. A perpetrator is afraid of a situation and reacts violently. Many, many times, they did not walk into a conversation planning to kill someone, yet they do.

How much investment in fear, pain, and anxiety

has to build up in a person before they "suddenly" kill another person? How much investment in fear, pain, and anxiety has to build up in a person before they yell and scream at someone they love and care about or hit or beat their child? How much investment in fear, pain, and anxiety has to build up in a person before they stop overeating, drinking, taking drugs to dull the pain of the fear? Unresolved, fear that festers exists as the genesis of violence, addiction, and dissatisfied living. We must resolve our fears, or we also can find ourselves suddenly doing something to ourselves or another person that we regret.

Strengthen Your Inner Immune System

1. Begin to look fear directly in the eyes. Where in your life can you see that you have been allowing fear to win?

2. Identify fears you have overcome in life. As children, we may have been afraid of the dark, or of clowns, or of certain people. Look at the story of these fears and notice what had to change for you to overcome them? Did more knowledge help? Did evolving or maturing in some way make the difference? Did you take a risk and step boldly forward?

The lymphatic system supports us by releasing toxins that find their way into our bodies from various sources. In the same way, our mind and awareness get flooded with toxic ideas about how afraid we should be every day. Whether watching the news, driving, thinking about our children's future, or undertaking any number of activities, we can feel the flood of toxins stress our awareness daily. We must learn to release these toxins from the past, present, and future effectively to be able to live courageously.

ToxiC
ReleasE

The Lymphatic System

The lymphatic system transports lymph, a fluid containing infection-fighting white blood cells, throughout the body. When this system works, our health thrives and our bodies achieve balance. Conversely, when this system is compromised or overwhelmed, we can become ill. In our world today, we are exposed to toxins frequently. We are blessed that our lymphatic system comes to the rescue.

Toxic Fear from Our Past

Due to the unconscious and unprocessed energy living in our deep mind, we often look at life through the lens of our past. While this can serve us in many respects, it also can cause us pain and create limitations.

Memories from our deep mind can be toxic to us. If we had some intense experience in our past that has not been healed, let go of, or forgiven, it will continue to influence our energy in our current experience. Our choices, perceptions, and relation-ships might be steeped in toxic fear. Most of us are unaware of this influence yet find ourselves with anxiety or an inability to think straight or take action, which can feel confusing. Such anxiety can be an indication that we are under the influence of some deep memory.

Those who serve or served in the military are not the only beings to experience post-traumatic stress disorder. After any traumatic experience, like a snake being thrown on you, there can be a triggered reaction from the past that rises fully intact with the accom-panying emotions, physical pain, or anxiety.

Many people just learn to live with these trig-gers and attempt to avoid situations to manage their fears from the past. However, there are ways for us to release even the most toxic memories and still remember them without being triggered into fear by them.

Toxic Fear in Our Now

The constant beat of the fear drum in our culture can be a toxin that triggers the fear stored in our deep mind. This can mean our entire system gets flooded with a double dose of frequent toxic fear. The stories about the bad news in our world and the constant rumblings of violence and the break-down of systems and respectful communications or actions express the beating of the fear drum. People around us might even be afraid for us about where we are headed or the actions we are taking. We might also feel the persistent fear most people experience as they reach for a better life in their own daily experience.

Toxic Fear of the Future

Motivating people with fear of the future can be a popular strategy. We have all heard admonitions from our parents about things we needed to be mindful of lest we influence our future in a negative way. The news fills us with stories about a bleak future if we don't change now. What is seen and perceived in the moment appears to absolutely predict the future.

Using fear as a motivator for the future tends to be ineffective. Still, worry about what might happen can be a habitual toxic and often-used thought pattern.

Daily Toxin Intake

The exposure to toxins, germs, and diseases can be invisible to our eye. This can also be true of the toxins the mind faces. Often, we have become so used to the voice of fear in our world that its overwhelming cackle blends into the daily noise of our living. Without some form of mental lymph, we begin to align, live from, and believe our toxic and fear-based thoughts.

Feeling Frozen

Observing when we freeze up might be one way we can see the takeover of toxic fear. We experience this feeling of being frozen if we are unable to make decisions or take action in some direction our mind might want us to go. It might feel like a desire to move toward some good, as we talk about it with others, yet doing nothing—classic procrastination. It might look like debilitating anxiety that makes it difficult to even get up and get going each day with the easiest of daily tasks.

Being frozen is a sure sign of the fear flu.

Impacting
Our Sense of Worth

Toxic fear eats away at our sense of self-worth. Every time this toxin wins out in our awareness it is like we got an inner shout down. This toxin eats away at our confidence in ourselves and life. When we are not confidant, our choices are impacted tremendously. We might reach for substances, people, and conditions that are harmful but that we believe deep down are all we are worthy of. The lower our sense of worth, the lower such choices will be. This cycle causes us to act from fear, experience more fear, and continue to be afraid to live and thrive.

Ability to Dream BIG

Most humans imagine many things about their ideal lives. Yet when fear is the core of their consciousness, moving toward such dreams can seem impossible. Pervasive fear also contributes to simply abandoning any desire to express—let alone accomplish—dreams. Resentment and bitterness then become core energies that motivate our choices. Why dream big at all? Nothing can ever come of it!

The story we tell ourselves might then be that only lucky people get to live their ideal lives. Or only people whom some God has blessed get to live great lives.

The fear toxin kills dreams.

Toxic Thoughts: Be Gone!

We cannot simply wish away our toxic thoughts or wave a magic wand at them. It takes a conscious strategy to begin to live in a way that our exposure to such toxic thoughts is decreased—and our ability to let go of our toxic thoughts consciously is embraced. Yet sometimes we are quite attached to the toxic fears we harbor. They are a part of us. Our fears can become part of our identity.

Trapped in Our Own Mind

We may be operating in what is akin to automatic pilot. In this state we may not even see the evidence of our fear. We might even argue with someone who tries to point it out or put down a book that suggests we are living in fear. Don't put this book down!

Fear toxin may simply become the normal way we respond to life. We are used to it and begin to feel that this is just the way we are. We are unaware that we are trapped in our toxic reality. In the book *Illusions*, author Richard Bach states, "Argue for your limitations, and they are yours." Our automatic pilot perceptions may cause us to argue vehemently for our limitations; yet it just might be fear toxin winning out.

Knowing We Can, Yet We Don't

If we did everything in life that we KNOW would be good for us, we would be golden. Even though each one of us often knows what serves us best—what is good and good for us—we may not do it all. Often the reason is toxic fear. We fall into a pattern of habitually feeding our fear rather than feeding ourselves a healthy and whole life. We fall into fear rather than taking a risk. We feed our fears and starve our courage.

There is a story about an elderly Cherokee man teaching his grandson about life. "A fight is going on inside me," he said to the boy. "It is a terrible fight and it is between two wolves. One is evil—he is anger, envy, sorrow, regret, greed, arrogance, self-pity, guilt, resentment, inferiority, lies, false pride, superiority, and ego."

He continued, "The other is good. He is joy, peace, love, hope, serenity, humility, kindness, benevolence, empathy, generosity, truth, compassion, and faith. The same fight is going on inside you—and inside every other person, too."

The grandson thought about it for a minute and then asked his grandfather, "Which wolf will win?" The grandfather replied, "The one I feed."

A Subtle, Yet Persistent Nudge

Even in the unhealthiest body, the ideal of health still can be sensed and felt in our awareness. Even though we may fall prey to the fear flu, some part of us can still feel the ideal of who we are and the life we could be living. We may be tempted to push it way down deep, yet the call of our highest and greatest self is a persistent truth in the human experience.

This dissonance can motivate us into a new idea and, therefore, a new life. If we let it.

To transcend toxicity requires us to consciously continue to use our intention with attention. First, we intend to heal a fear. Then we use attention in some way to habitually move in that direction.

In 1991, at the age of twenty-seven, I faced the worst fear of my life up to that point. I left my lifelong home state of Colorado to move to Southern California and experienced a thrilling time of newness. I felt great joy as I launched my ministerial life. New work, new home, new friends had me full of excitement. Yet, one unique thing about that area of the world is the presence of earthquakes, which I had never experienced before. I had grown up with knee deep, windy, slippery snowfalls and below-zero temperatures during winter. But the idea of the earth shaking below my feet and home caused a profound sense of fear and anxiety to rise up in me.

In 1994 the Northridge Earthquake startled me awake at four a.m. as it rumbled through Southern

California. My two-story condo shook like it would collapse. As I stood in a doorway and gazed out the back window on the second floor, I wondered, "Might the safest place for me to be on that second floor such that if the house collapsed, I would be on top of the rubble? Or should I go downstairs and hide under a table such that the house could collapse around me?" I was petrified and deeply alone in my fear.

After my condo and I survived that earthquake, debilitating fear and anxiety followed me everywhere I went. As I drove down a road I wondered where I could pull off in the instance of an earthquake. When I entered a store, movie theater, or restaurant, I wondered what door I would use if there were an earthquake. Earthquakes consumed my thoughts. I looked at every location through earthquake-colored eyes and nervous system.

Finally, feeling that I could not possibly live the rest of my life this afraid all the time, I knew I had to do something. In desperation and exasperation, and with an intention to heal my fear, I called my mother for help. Together we devised a plan for me to feel less afraid.

I placed my attention on my material word as the first part of the plan. I created some practical support for myself to feel a greater sense of safety. I put together a kit for my car and a kit at home with supplies such as food, water, blankets, and extra tennis shoes. I learned about the utilities in my home and what to do with them in an emergency. These things helped me feel more physically secure.

Still, I do not believe that the power to control Mother Earth or pray the earthquakes away is mine. The Earth has to do what she has to do to maintain her balance. I did realize that on numerous occasions calmness led me right where I needed to be with great synchronicity. This may, in fact, be one of my superpowers! So, I created an affirmation for myself. This is a positive statement of how I choose to be or experience some aspect of life. My affirmation went like this: "I am always in the right time at the right place to ensure my total safety."

I began to use my affirmation regularly. Instead of obsessing about what I would do during an earthquake when I drove, I recited my affirmation. I spoke it aloud when I was at home. Any time I felt any bit of fear arise, I said or thought the affirmation.

It took a few months, yet eventually the fear began to subside dramatically.

Confirmation of the alleviation of the fear for good dawned on me one night while home alone on my couch when the earth quaked again. I found myself sitting there peacefully with my cat in my lap, watching the earth and my condo move, feeling peaceful and curious. I asked my innermost self if I needed to run for cover and got a clear, "NO!" Then, the shaking stopped, and life resumed.

Release Toxic Thoughts

1. Notice your "stinking thinking." Where do your toxic thoughts tend to focus? Consider taking a break from them. For example, if watching the news always creates

a pattern of toxicity, take a break from the news for a period of time.

2. Create an affirmation for yourself about any toxic fear that persistently arises. Feel free to use my earthquakes-busting affirmation, if it suits you.

Bone marrow flows through our bones, the structure of our bodies, as the primary site of new blood cell production. When we successfully learn to release toxic thoughts and begin to consciously practice courage and faith, there is a new strength that emerges as the structure of our living. The embrace of meaningful paths to courage in the face of any fear is a powerful practice that heroes and "she-roes" throughout history have exemplified. In our world, we are each called to embrace this powerful bone marrow for our soul.

CouragE
Is
BonE MarroW

Living as Courage and Faith

The reality of our lives is that every day we are faced with the choice to let fear win or let courage and faith win. Courage and faith are the natural living waters of our essence. When we let fear win, we are literally not in our right mind or our right self. Our habits of mind and awareness may habitually tune into station K-F-E-A-R and react from that signal over and over.

Are You . . . Chicken?

In the movie *Back to the Future,* Michael J. Fox's character habitually reacted to being called a chicken. Other characters in the movie knew that they could get a reaction out of "Marty" if they just taunted him with that one word. They could manipulate him with his fear of appearing to be afraid. While this is humorous in the movie, in our daily lives it is amazing to awaken to our automatic habits that words, conditions, and people trigger.

Courage Every Day

While we may be tempted to let fear rule the day, all the while the bone marrow of courage pours through our awareness. We don't give ourselves enough credit for the courage we express every day of our lives. It is courageous to be and do most of what we are being and doing. This being human and mortal on planet Earth is a courageous existence, given that the outcome is ensured: None of us are getting out of this alive in our current body or life.

Waking UP!

When we start to focus on the courage already present in us and the courage we want to cultivate, we begin to expand in our awareness and experience. The way our brain works, the more we focus in a certain direction, the more our brain helps us see what we are choosing to focus on—whether it is positive or negative.

Our brain is like an extremely sophisticated search

engine. In the world of the internet, if we open a search engine and type in a word, articles, photos, and videos related to that word show up. If the word is "relationships," we will see a whole bunch of things related to that topic.

If we put the word "relationships" in a search engine and then add the word "fear" to the search, the tone of the search would shift, based on that added word. All sorts of things emerge about why we should be afraid in our relationships. News stories about relationships gone horribly wrong would emerge.

A search engine is like the eyes we can see our world through and the result we get is completely connected to the quality and tone of our search. This is also how our brain works, how our perception of the world works. Yes, there are bad and challenging things going on in our world. Yet there are also glorious, amazing, miraculous, and life-affirming things going on in our world. The quality of our perceptions is totally related to the quality of our search or perception.

This is why the first step to healing fear is to wake up from the fear and begin to use our intentionality and ability to focus our attention—to choose to see our courage and the courage that flows through the bone marrow of humanity despite negative conditions or experiences.

This is the pivot countless humans make to step forward and claim a greater life. No matter what has happened, is happening, or will happen, our courageous spirit is bigger than any condition we may face.

Stories of Courage

We can become greatly inspired when we study and reflect on the lives of courageous beings we admire. There are many, many more stories of beings who have been and are being strong and courageous than there are stories of fear winning out. Because the fear stories win ratings and attention in our culture, they are louder and appear to be more pervasive. The truth is there are more good, more effective, more powerful acts happening everywhere than we realize. Reading and reflecting on them every day counter-acts the effects of fear.

Example 1: OPRAH

Celebrity and media mogul Oprah Winfrey represents a classic example of a person whose challenging past could completely define their future. Born into poverty and pain, abused and neglected in the most horrific ways humans abuse and neglect one another, she found that deep inside her lived dreams and possibilities. Though she experienced challenging conditions as a child—and many of the older people in her life treated her unkindly, absent of any generosity in their actions—like all of us, she encountered some good and kind people around her who chose to encourage and care for her. At some point, she made a choice to listen to those encouraging voices instead of her painful past.

On the surface we might think she is successful because of her wealth or celebrity status. Yet, her courage is that of challenging the establishments of our culture and stepping up as a Black woman to create an "out-of-the-box" talk show that helped and supported millions of viewers. She could have chosen to play small in life—and given her past, no one would blame her. Yet she transcended her past and chose to play big.

Example 2: JESUS

This master teacher welcomed the limelight instead of quietly and privately sharing his stories with anyone who would listen. He could have laid low. Yet, the gospels tell us that Jesus courageously listened to an inner voice that guided him in his life and ministry, even to his death. What lived in him that caused him to listen to this voice? How did he embrace the courage to experience such suffering and even death?

The stories written about him indicate a life lived with an obedience to a deep inner voice that became a trusted voice of truth for Jesus. The courage of this trust has stood the test of time and inspired countless followers to live more courageously from many faith traditions.

Example 3: MY MOM

My own mother is the most courageous person I know—other than that whole snake phobia. Having gotten pregnant with me as a teenager and marrying my rage-a-holic father, ending up with three kids before the age of twenty-three, and living a challenging early married life, my mother had tremendous courage to walk out of that marriage with her three kids and virtually no money into a new life. It took her fourteen years to drum up the courage, yet she did it. She also began diligent personal growth work to become a stronger version of herself for her own life and for her children. She transformed into a wonderful provider, business owner, international speaker, and now is a private practitioner, helping people learn how to live their best lives.

She is the reason that I am sure transformation of anyone with any past or any fear is totally possible. Witnessing this with my own eyes is powerful. When we choose to courageously face ourselves, our past, and our hidden beliefs and heal them, we can move mountains.

Bone Marrow for Our Soul

In the immune system, bone marrow, which is a semi-solid tissue found in the spongy portions of bones, is the primary site of new blood cell production. These healthy cells are then circulated and contribute to the health of our body. When our mind and awareness become focused habitually on inspirational stories of courage, it is like healthy consciousness cells are circulated into our awareness. This provides a new undercurrent of courage and possibility for us.

If They Can, I Can

When we read, study, and remind ourselves of stories of people overcoming the odds we may have faced, we find encouragement and hope. Something deep inside us that knows who we truly are and what we are truly capable of is stirred. We might feel that sense that if other people can walk through as great or even greater challenges than we have, there may be hope for us. And there is hope for us. At the very least, we may become curious about how the courageous ones overcame the odds, and that curiosity is an opening that allows the emotional bone marrow of courage to begin to course through our being.

Science has been studying mirror neurons in the brain for a number of years. While there is some controversy about their existence and the role they play, experiments in this field of study suggest that mirror neurons help us imitate others. Whether learning a skill or having empathy, our brain may be attempting to imitate others around us.

In the May 1, 2015, issue of *Scientific American,* Harvard University Professor Srini Pillay is quoted as saying, "Studies have shown that the same brain regions become active when a person performs a task and when a person observes someone carrying out a task. But mirror neurons may have an even more complex part than recording others' movements; these neurons may help explain our capacity for empathy."

If true, this could explain part of why we feel inspired when we see others doing things we would like to be doing. Even if mirror neurons are not the reason or don't exist, watching others be courageous seems like it can only be a good thing for our brain and for us.

Emotional Integrity
IS Possible

Integrity is synonymous with wholeness. When something is whole, it is available in its totality. Living from fear is living from our brokenness, and when we cannot see beyond our brokenness, it can be challenging to even consider our wholeness. Yet living examples of other humans who have done the inner work to heal their fear and step into a life of wholeness inspire us. It is not that those lives are perfect lives without challenges. It is that those lives are lived with courage such that when something to fear shows up, they are more able to respond and react with courage and faith to walk forward through it rather than getting stuck in it.

Inspired
Into Who I Really Am

Who we really are is a being fully equipped to meet the challenges of life head on. Who we really are is strong, creative, guided, powerful, and courageous. No matter what horrific things have happened in the human realm, there are always beings who demonstrate who we really are as a human being. Those stories touch us and are soul stirring because they reflect the truth about us.

Once we have sensed that truth, we can lead ourselves back to the waters of that truth anytime we want to or need to. The question then becomes: Will we?

Up-Level Your Bone Marrow

1. Keep track of moments of courage in a computer file or journal. Choose stories through history or your family history that inspire you to be courageous. Spend time reading these stories and give gratitude for the courageous souls represented in them.

2. Consider keeping a list of your personal moments of courage in the same file. Reflect on those regularly. We all need to be reminded that we can be courageous.

In our bodies, the spleen acts primarily as a blood filter and plays an important role in producing red blood cells and supporting our immune system.

Like the red blood cells that flow through our bodies, what is in our consciousness or awareness flows through every part of our being and impacts our energy and decisions. The primary place where opportunities exist for us to begin to make new courageous choices is in a deeper sense of our spiritual connection to everything and everyone. When we live life feeling connected, we experience a powerful sense of confidence and serenity that begins to allow us to transcend our fear. Fearless living becomes our norm.

GeT a SpirituaL SpleeN

What's In Your Consciousness?

Just as the body constantly reflects its current state of health and its needs that we can see and feel, our consciousness is the seat of circulation for the totality of our life. Fear would have us separate ourselves from our challenges. It gives us the opportunity to play the victim and feel separate from conditions we experience. This cannot help us solve any of the problems we face.

To solve our challenges and fear, we must be and think like our immune system does when it encounters unhealthy cells: Face them, embrace them, and transform them.

Facing Our Fears

There is a developmental phase for toddlers where if something or someone is not in their sight, their brains think it no longer exists. Like toddlers, we humans have persisted in thinking that when it comes to our inner pains and emotional experiences, if it is over or we are not in the space of it, it no longer exists. Yet transcending anything requires us to look right at it and name it.

Learning to face our fears and see that we can survive facing them helps us continue to develop courage. This courage circulates through us and gives us strength and inspiration to heal that which we are afraid of.

Embracing Our Fears

Embracing our fears may seem counterintuitive. Embracing our fears is like loving our enemy. There is an alchemical shift that begins to happen when we fully embrace fear. Embracing our fears includes telling someone about them, journaling about our fears, crying about our fears, or feeling our fears and doing whatever we're afraid of anyway.

The goal of this embrace is to fully own that we have been or are feeling fear. We no longer deny it.

We acknowledge it in some way that is meaningful for us. As we own the fear, the clarity about where it came from and exactly how it has been serving us may begin to dawn on us.

Transforming Our Fears

In the space of loving compassion for ourselves and the part of us that has been living in fear, we can begin to transform fear into faith. We can see there has been a good reason that our fear was there. It sought to keep us safe or protect us. Witnessing this, we can begin to thank it and let it go. We can literally direct our awareness to let go of fear or, at the very least, understand that while we may still feel afraid, we are going to move forward. We are going to proceed in faith—faith in ourselves and our lives. No matter what, we are going to do fine and be fine. If we are not fine, we can figure it out.

Fear no longer rules our decisions.

One of the reasons we tend to gravitate toward

stories with superheroes in them is that we love to see the good person win. We also see that most such beings, when faced with a crisis, find they already have everything they need to win. Batman pulls just the right tool out of his skintight bat suit; Harry Potter has just the right spell; Iron Man figures it out or fights it out just right.

These stories resonate for many of us because they are the truth of us. We have what we need to meet any challenge we face. The more we begin to see this and believe this, the more we see it as the truth. And then the question becomes, "Why would we ever need to be afraid?"

Oneness and Our Connection

In every faith tradition on our planet there are those who enter the mystical realms. They may consciously pray themselves there, or they may suddenly find themselves there. When this occurs, we find there are common themes or experiences that have emerged throughout time. The themes point to a deep sense of feeling one with all things and all people, a recognition that who we are contributes to everything, and a great sense of partnership with God or the Universe. The embrace of deeper faith can lead us powerfully into this mystical awareness.

Feeling One

The feeling of oneness with all things and people can bring forth a great sense of confidence to proceed with life in its fullness. This is a truly empowered feeling. This feeling helps us understand that we are not ever alone, which is a popular thing to feel, and that we can proceed and even take risks to pursue our dreams.

When we feel this and ask ourselves, "What is the worst that can happen?," we begin to see that even if most of the scenarios of fear we imagined did come true, still we could handle it, figure it out, deal with it, get help, or survive. The resources we need to solve our challenges are readily available to us—

and this becomes so clear in the midst of feeling connected.

A Constant Broadcast

Because we are connected energetically to everyone and everything, we contribute to everyone and everything. When we cease broadcasting fear, fear, and more fear, we can become a positive contribution to the places and people we share our life with. This creates somewhat of a snowball effect. When someone who participates in a group constantly expresses fear, they impact the group experience, just as someone participating in a group with ease and grace impacts the group.

Every time we heal a fear or a pain, we continue our journey to becoming a person of increase because our broadcast is transformed. This personal growth work is not just for us or to make our lives better. The better, fearless self we can be is inspirational to others and is good for the world.

A Divine Partnership

We begin to see a synchronicity emerge. The truth is that synchronicity is part of living, even when we are living from fear. Our partnership with the Divine is active, whether we are using it to play small or play big. When we are living from fear, it is as if we are a match for our brain and our life to show us proof that we should keep being afraid.

Conversely, choosing to be free of fear flu and instead embrace faith means that our brains and our lives begin to show us proof about how we can remain fearless. It can literally feel like a partnership, or magic, yet it is how life works. Try it out—I dare you!

Fearless Living

There is a foundation of trust and faith in oneself and life in general that emerges when we lead ourselves repeatedly back to an embrace of our true source. This is different than just thinking about it. Living this way requires a profound and habitual conscious choice to enter the Divine realms of our consciousness and lay our fears and concerns on the altar of our Oneness. Fear may still emerge or become triggered, of course, but who we become and how we react in the midst of fear changes forever.

Fears
that Matter

Once again, if we are in a situation that is dangerous to our safety, fear is appropriate and helpful to propel us forward. If we are being physically hurt or abused in any way, if we are participating in acts that could harm our body or health, if there is a truck headed right for us, the launch of fear can save our lives. The more we embody our Oneness, the more we can begin to experience what might be a precognitive kind of fear that warns us not to drive a certain street, or get on that plane, or go off with that stranger.

Over the years I have learned to trust my intuition. I am obedient to that little inner voice, the gut reaction that encourages me to "go left now" as I drive. It is the same voice I use to manage my fear.

Flying on airplanes brings on bouts of fear flu for many people. Some literally will not fly out of such a fear. They don't travel or go to their dream destinations because the plane might crash. As I grow older, I am obedient to the little inner voice because if it ever tells me not to get on a plane, I won't. But I am careful also to distinguish between the centered part of me that speaks from my depth and my fear voice. Being in touch with my highest self and leaning into the synchronicity of life help me recognize the difference.

Fears
of the Unknown

Often we cling to fear as we approach a situation with many unknowns. Yet, if we reflect on our days, we begin to see that we walk forward into the unknown more than the known every single day. Even though we may venture into familiar environments and relationships every day of our lives, we never know exactly what will be said. There will be elements we cannot predict about the encounters we have.

When we begin to see and embrace this reality, we can make peace with our obsession about the unknown and even begin to appreciate it.

Fears
We Imagine

If our imagination takes off on us like an out-of-control horse, we must begin to see that we hold the reigns of that horse. Our imagination is ours, and we can stop it, change it, shift it at will. It is not something that controls us; we control it. Only if we surrender control will we find ourselves heading down a path we prefer not to head down. Just being able to stop and say to ourselves, "Whoa, where is THAT fear coming from?," can allow us to begin to open up our awareness and start the healing journey back to courage and faith.

Plug Into Your Power

1. If your worst fear came true right now, what is the worst that could happen? If the worst that could happen happened, how might it impact you? Look right at it and see if even though the worst case you can imagine might be frustrating, inconvenient, unpleasant, yet could you survive and thrive again even if it happened?

2. Take a deep breath and sense the wisest part of your deepest self. How does this part of you think you could and should approach or deal with this fear?

White blood cells only account for one percent of our blood, yet they have a huge impact on how our bodies function. They protect us from illness and disease as they rush in to help destroy any harmful substances.

When we have made a practice out of bathing our awareness in high ideas based in ease, grace, and light, our consciousness becomes inoculated against the fear virus. We become immune to the world's insistence that we live in fear. Our lives become empowered. We begin to create more and more of what we want—and less and less of what we don't want.

WhitE LighT
CellS

Practices of Light

We might imagine that the challenges of fear are so large that we would have to sit on our prayer mats chanting mantras all day every day to transform our experiences. This imagining can be an excuse to do nothing, in which case our lives will remain just as they were.

Yet, like the white blood cells that make up a small portion of our blood and have a huge impact on our health, we can make a huge difference with daily disciplines that take a brief amount time and have an outsized and lasting impact. This impact can affect our entire being as we find ourselves less focused on fear and its triggers and more able to live from courage.

Forgive

Every faith tradition teaches forgiveness. Forgiveness frees us. When we truly forgive the harm, hurt, betrayal, or teachings of dysfunctional ways of living, we free ourselves to return to our original programming of courage and faith. Each time we move thorough forgiveness we "un-Earth" the hold of fear.

Speak Truth

When our fears remain secret, they fester in our hearts, souls, and consciousnesses. On discovering a trustworthy source with whom we speak our truth about what we fear and why we fear it, a new opportunity emerges for partnership in freedom. This trusted source might be our best friend, counsellor, coach, or family member. Amazing opportunities to feel heard, seen, and supported emerge with such sharing. Courage and faith are restored.

Meditate

Research about the benefits of meditation demonstrate that these benefits show up in every realm of life for those who meditate regularly. Healing the fear flu with meditation exposes us to a perception of our true source of power. This aspect of self—often called the Higher Self, soul, or essence—guides us profoundly. To be in touch with it allows us to unlock the secrets to our own healing pathway.

Inoculating Our Consciousness

The whole goal of inoculations is to protect us from the experience of disease, as well as to prevent us from being a carrier of that disease. While there is a lot of controversy and even fear about inoculations for our body, the idea of it for our awareness is a great metaphor.

When we enter into practices of light on a regular basis, we begin to be immune to fear. We cease being a carrier of the virus into our thoughts, relationships, bodies, workplaces, locations, and homes. We become a healthy cell in the body of the universe.

Fasting from Fear

As with all new endeavors we undertake, we must consciously choose to let go of the old and embrace the new. A choice to cease feeding our fear must emerge in order for us to be successful. We might see this as a fast, or a diet from a way of being, thinking and feeling that no longer serves us. As fear emerges, we can take a deep breath and remind ourselves that we are fasting from fear—just for this week, or this day, or this hour. All healing takes self-awareness and self-direction.

Managing Our Mind

Becoming present to the shenanigans of our mind cultivates self-awareness. Otherwise our mind can take off thinking like a freight train jumping the tracks. We can end up in places we don't want to be.

Using cues, timers, journals, or moments of reflecting on our thoughts are all extremely helpful in awakening to our thought tendencies. We must learn not to believe everything we think.

Managing Our Mouth

Our thoughts and words are the building blocks of our lives. Paying attention to how many times we tell ourselves or another to be afraid serves us in ending that pattern. Ending that pattern allows us to find ways to speak that are up-lifting. Managing how often we share about the scary things we see, experience, or feel concern about can be life changing. What we say shows us what we are focused on. What we are focused on becomes our experience.

A Life that Works for Everyone, Including Me

The idea of creating a life that works for everyone is the major intention of the Centers for Spiritual Living. This notion creates a range of responses, from positive feelings to criticism to discussion. This big and broad idea can only come into reality when fear is no longer at the core of our experience as human beings.

Creating a world that works for everyone supposes

that there is a way we can all live our best lives—and that if that came true, there would be a pervasive harmony. Arguing with this idea as a possibility is one way our fear speaks as we wonder if the life someone else wants might infringe on our life negatively.

Fear Is Not Working for Us

If focusing on fear truly worked, our planet would be in a much better place. Habitual fear does not make us happier, healthier, or even safer. Habitual fear makes us more afraid, less happy, less healthy, and causes us to make poor choices. The deeper power within us provides our safe place. Learning to access and rely on this makes our life truly safe.

My Healthy Life

Inoculating and insulating ourselves from habitual fear may feel foreign and strange at first. Just as when we start a new way of eating, or exercise, or any other endeavor feels foreign at first. These new ways of being ultimately bring us greater health and well-being, as does fearless living. We find ourselves able to meet the challenges we face with calm and assurance. We solve problems, deal with concerns, and meet challenges from a profoundly confident place. True solutions of ease, grace, and peace emerge.

What I Want for Me, I Want for You

As this new way of living seeps into our daily life and the benefits of it manifest, we may find we want this way of life for all beings. Imagine a world of calm and confident beings living in calm and confidence about their ability to meet the challenges and problems of their lives. With fear decreasing dramatically, force, violence, and most of the things we fear can fall away. Issues of our world, individually and collectively, can be dealt with in a space of reverence and respect.

> *"You may say I am a dreamer,*
> *but I'm not the only one."*

—JOHN LENNON

Let White Light Cells Flow

1. Are there beings you need to forgive to be free of resentments? Can you list their names and spend time each day sending them white light and love, therefore setting yourself free?

2. Identify a fear—or two—that, after reading this book, you plan to work on healing.

ThE EnD oF FeaR

Small Steps

Throughout this book there have been various personal stories—and stories of others about transcending fear. At the end of each chapter are questions designed to help explore where and how fear may impact daily living.

Moving beyond unnecessary fear often happens in small steps, taken one at a time. Rarely does anyone just decide to stop being afraid. That decision comes after a whole new mindset is built to replace previous fear-based thoughts and ideas.

Building Blocks

To shift any habit or mindset requires attention and intention. Just as a person who wants to improve health would begin with changing their habits with regard to their body, those who wish to change the level of their fear must make some new choices around their habits of mind and, often, actions. Each change becomes a building block that contributes to the whole experience of life.

The process can take time, effort, and awareness. Yet the benefits to our individual life and our contribution to humanity is profound—and well worth it if we wish to end the legacy of fear-based living.

Suggestions for New Habits

There are a number of steps we can take to begin to build a more courageous life. Creating an affirmation to say repeatedly that can help in daily life, or when fear rises, can be extremely powerful. The affirmation I created around earthquakes changed my life dramatically and continues to be a vital part of my own fear management.

Getting prayer support can help us feel connected and not so alone in our fear. Finding a faith tradition or having friends who will include us in their prayers can be a powerful way to let fear go. Knowing we are not alone and knowing someone sees us clearly in the challenge we face—and is willing to affirm and support us in making the change we desire—these feed our courageous hearts.

Getting help from professionals can be important. If we have fear that debilitates us, we can get help. There are therapists, counselors, phobia and fear specialists who have expertise to help us get beyond our fears. We can share our need for support with people and get recommendations, or we can use the power of the Internet to find experts.

Incorporating other ideas from this book can support the release of fear. Creating a courage journal, researching stories of people who have gotten beyond the fears we have, and other ideas suggested can be great companions to us in our embrace of greater courage.

One Last Thought

Let us remember that everyone faces fears. To feel fear or have fear about conditions or situations does not make us weak; it makes us human. When we have fear and then criticize ourselves or shame ourselves, we are not helping ourselves in any way to move beyond it. Such an approach actually anchors us in greater fear. When we can remember this and be gentle and kind to ourselves as we deal with our fears, we have a much greater chance of actually shifting away from fear and moving into a thriving state of being.

Each fear transformed empowers us to deal with any others already present or that show up. Indeed, having fear in certain areas can indicate that we care, that we want to do well, that we want to live more fully.

Be gentle—and lovingly move beyond the fears that may have stopped you in the past.

AbouT
the AuthoR

Rev. Dr. Michelle Medrano is a career minister in the New Thought movement. She received her ministerial degree at the School of Ministry at Mile Hi Church in 1991. The Huntington Beach Church of Religious Science hired her as an assistant minister, and she served in that capacity for four years. Then she was blessed to serve as senior minister of New Vision Center for seventeen years. In 2013, she was invited back to Mile Hi to serve as an associate minister. In the spring of 2019, she joined Rev. Joshua Reeves as the co-lead minister of Mile Hi Church. Writing runs in her family and authoring articles and books has been a part of her career dreams for a long time. This is her first book.

Made in the USA
Las Vegas, NV
11 May 2022

48773042R00058